my first picture dictionary

Anne Civardi

Illustrated by
Graham Philpot
Consultant: Betty Root

Bounty
Books

All about this dictionary

This colourful, highly amusing picture dictionary will be enjoyed by all young children. The very young will love to share it with an adult, turning over the pages and talking about the delightful and lively pictures. They will have great fun discovering The Word Gang – Ollie Octopus, Millie Mouse, Patsy Pig, Boris Bear and all their friends – who appear throughout the book getting up to all sorts of antics while helping to illustrate the meaning of the words.

Those children who have just started to read will not find the text difficult because great care has been taken to ensure that the pictures give the right clues to the sentences underneath. The sentences put the words into context and in association with the pictures convey their meaning.

As it is a first word book, only nouns and verbs have been used. The nouns are in **grey** print and the verbs in **blue**. It will be helpful to explain to children that words which are the names of people and things are called nouns. Words that tell you what the animals are doing are called verbs.

Because this is a dictionary, the words are in alphabetical order. By using this book frequently, children will begin to learn where letters occur in the alphabet. This is a very important skill which will help them in many ways.

My First Picture Dictionary has outstanding and very original illustrations, and because of the humour, the colour and the content, children will want to return to it again and again. Through the joy of using it they will learn lots of new words and how to read and spell them.

Betty Root

Reading and Language Consultant
University of Reading

Noun
kangaroo

Kelly is a **kangaroo**.

Verb
blowing

Millie Mouse is **blowing** out the candle.

The Word Gang

This is The Word Gang. Look for these animals in the book and find out what each of them gets up to.

abcdefghijklmnopqrstuvwxyz

Aa

alphabet

The first letter of the **alphabet** is a.

animals
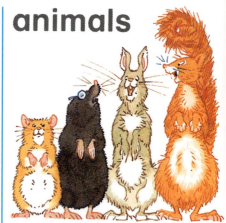
Four furry **animals** standing in a row.

aeroplane

Derek Duck is flying the **aeroplane**.

ambulance

The **ambulance** is going to the hospital.

ants
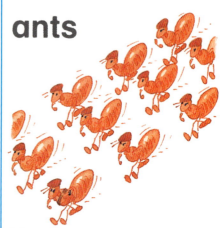
Marching red **ants**.

airport

Derek Duck is landing at the **airport**.

angel

The **angel** is singing.

apple

Willie Worm is eating a green **apple**.

abcdefghijklmnopqrstuvwxyz

apron

Patsy Pig is wearing a frilly **apron**.

Bb

bag
The brown **bag** is full of money.

arrow

The **arrow** has hit the tree trunk.

baby
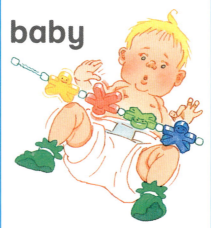
The **baby** is playing.

baker

The **baker** has baked a loaf of bread.

astronaut
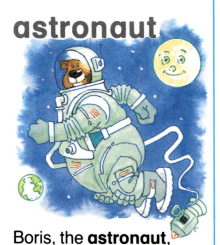
Boris, the **astronaut**, is floating in space.

badges

Gertie Giraffe has six coloured **badges**.

ball
Millie Mouse is walking on the **ball**.

5

a b c d e f g h i j k l m n o p q r s t u v w x y z

balloon

Millie Mouse is hanging on to the **balloon**.

band

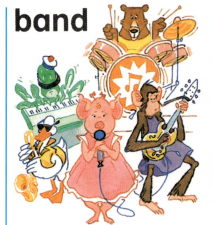

The animals are playing in the **band**.

bath

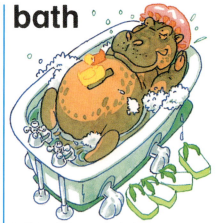

Hilda Hippo is lying in the **bath**.

basket

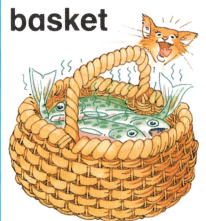

The **basket** is full of smelly fish.

beans

A plate of **beans**.

bananas

A big bunch of ripe, yellow **bananas**.

bat

Roger Rabbit has a baseball **bat**.

bear

Boris is a happy **bear**.

a**b**cdefghijklmnopqrstuvwxyz

bed
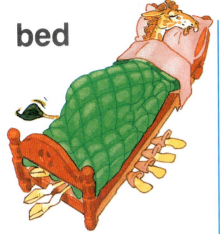
Gertie Giraffe has a very long **bed**.

belt

Boris Bear's red and yellow **belt**.

blowing

Millie Mouse is **blowing** out the candle.

bee

The **bee** gets honey from the flower.

bicycle

Molly Monkey is riding her **bicycle**.

boat

Ollie Octopus is rowing the **boat**.

bell

Millie Mouse is ringing the **bell**.

bird

Bill is a big **bird**.

bone

Dudley Dog has a big, juicy **bone**.

a**b**cdefghijklmnopqrstuvwxyz

book

Willie Worm is busy reading his **book**.

bottom
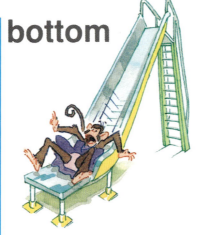
Molly Monkey is at the **bottom** of the slide.

boy

Jake is a **boy**.

boot

A big, brown **boot**.

bowl

A **bowl** of hot porridge for Boris Bear.

branch

Two little birds on a big **branch**.

bottle

A **bottle** of fizzy beer.

box

Carly Cat is asleep in the **box**.

bread

Millie is nibbling a hole in the loaf of **bread**.

abcdefghijklmnopqrstuvwxyz

breakfast

Two eggs and toast for **breakfast**.

brick

Roger Rabbit is carrying a heavy **brick**.

bridge

The boat is going under the **bridge**.

brushing

Leo Lion is **brushing** his long mane.

bubble

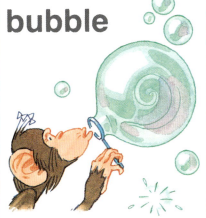

Molly Monkey is blowing a big, round **bubble**.

bucket

Freddie Frog peeps out of the **bucket**.

building

Bill Bird is **building** a big nest.

bull

An angry **bull**.

a b c d e f g h i j k l m n o p q r s t u v w x y z

bulldozer

Derek Duck is driving a yellow **bulldozer**.

butcher

The **butcher** is chopping up meat.

Cc

bus

The **bus** stops at the bus stop.

butter

Millie Mouse is smelling the **butter**.

cabbage

The tortoise likes eating lots of **cabbage**.

bush

A bird in a **bush**.

butterfly

A big, beautiful, blue **butterfly**.

cage

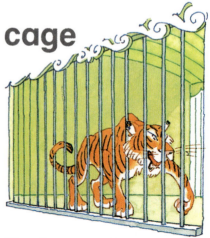

The tiger prowls around the **cage**.

ab**c**defghijklmnopqrstuvwxyz

cake

A big, chocolate **cake**.

camping
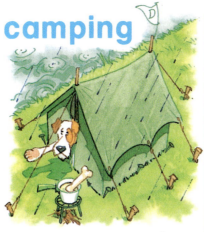
Dudley Dog is **camping** in the rain.

car

Derek Duck has a shiny yellow sports **car**.

camel

Derek Duck is riding a **camel**.

candle

There is one **candle** on the cake.

carpet
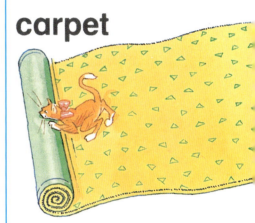
Carly Cat rolls out the **carpet**.

camera

Boris Bear takes pictures with his **camera**.

cap

Roger Rabbit is wearing a red **cap**.

carrot

Roger Rabbit munches on the big **carrot**.

abcdefghijklmnopqrstuvwxyz

castle

There is a moat around the **castle**.

cat
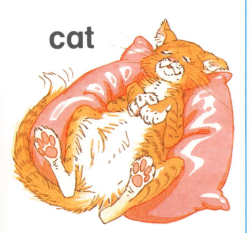
Carly is a sleepy **cat**.

catching

Roger Rabbit is **catching** the ball.

caterpillar

A big, green, hairy **caterpillar**.

cauliflower

Ellie Elephant has picked a **cauliflower**.

cave

A dark, spooky **cave**.

chair

Freddie Frog sits on the **chair**.

chasing

Carly Cat is **chasing** the mouse.

ab**c**defghijklmnopqrstuvwxyz

cheese

Millie Mouse loves eating **cheese**.

chicken

The **chicken** has laid a big, brown egg.

chocolate
Old Croc is eating a bar of **chocolate**.

cherries

The ripe **cherries** are on the branch.

children

The **children** are playing.

Christmas

Ollie Octopus gets lots of presents at **Christmas**.

chess

Willie and Millie are playing **chess**.

chimney
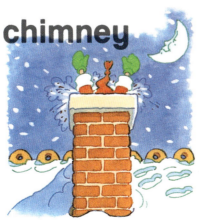
Santa Claus goes down the **chimney**.

church

The **church** is on top of the hill.

a b **c** d e f g h i j k l m n o p q r s t u v w x y z

circle

The ducks swim in a big **circle**.

clock

The cuckoo comes out of the **clock**.

coat

Boris Bear has a smart blue **coat**.

cleaning

Patsy Pig is **cleaning** the mirror.

cloud

Bill Bird flies through the **cloud**.

combing

Leo Lion is **combing** his long whiskers.

climbing

Molly Monkey is **climbing** up the rope.

clown

The **clown** is making a funny face.

comic
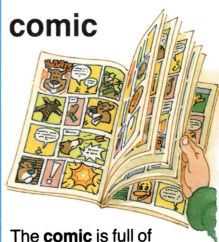
The **comic** is full of funny pictures.

ab**c**defghijklmnopqrstuvwxyz

computer

Molly Monkey is working on her **computer**.

cow

The brown **cow** has a little calf.

crane
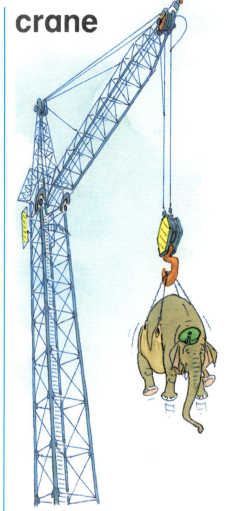
The **crane** lifts up Ellie Elephant.

cooking
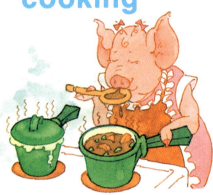
Patsy Pig is **cooking** dinner for Boris.

cowboy

Roger is pretending to be a **cowboy**.

counting

Boris Bear is **counting** his money.

crab

The **crab** is walking across the sand.

crashing

The cars are **crashing** into each other.

abcdefghijklmnopqrstuvwxyz

crayon

Millie Mouse is drawing with a red **crayon**.

crown

The king is wearing a golden **crown**.

cup

This is Boris Bear's best **cup**.

crocodile

Old Croc is a very old **crocodile**.

crying

Old Croc is **crying**.

curtain
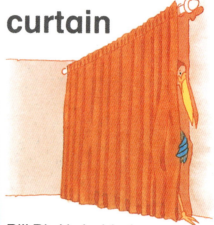
Bill Bird is behind the **curtain**.

crossing

Kelly Kangaroo is **crossing** the road.

cucumber

Roger Rabbit is slicing the **cucumber**.

cutting

Molly Monkey is busy **cutting** the hedge.

abc**d**efghijklmnopqrstuvwxyz

Dd

dancing

Patsy Pig loves **dancing** with Boris Bear.

deer

The **deer** has spiky antlers on his head.

daffodils

A beautiful bunch of yellow **daffodils**.

dark

It is **dark** outside.

dentist

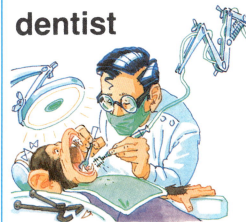

The **dentist** is mending Molly Monkey's teeth.

dancer

Patsy Pig wants to be a famous **dancer**.

deep

Freddie Frog is swimming in **deep** water.

desert

It is very hot and dry in the **desert**.

abc**d**efghijklmnopqrstuvwxyz

desk

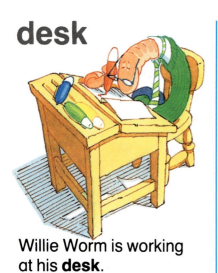

Willie Worm is working at his **desk**.

digging

Dudley Dog is **digging** a deep hole.

dinosaur

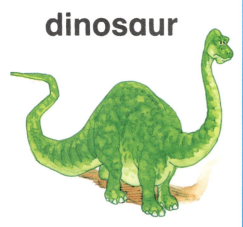

A big, green **dinosaur**.

diving

Freddie Frog is **diving** off a high rock.

doctor

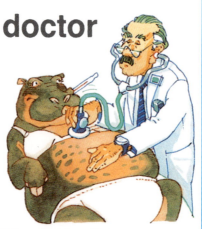

The **doctor** listens to Hilda Hippo's heart.

dog

Dudley is a dirty **dog**.

doll

The **doll** has lots of curly red hair.

dolphin

The **dolphin** is jumping out of the water.

abc**d**efghijklmnopqrstuvwxyz

donkey

Roger Rabbit is riding on a **donkey**.

drawing
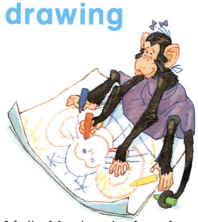
Molly Monkey is **drawing** a picture of herself.

driving

Derek Duck is **driving** his new sports car.

door

Ellie Elephant opens the **door** with her trunk.

dress

Patsy Pig is wearing her favourite **dress**.

drum

Boris Bear beats the big **drum**.

dragon

The **dragon** has wings and breathes fire.

drinking

Molly Monkey is **drinking** a glass of orange juice.

duck

Derek is a busy **duck**.

abcdefghijklmnopqrstuvwxyz

Ee

eating

Boris Bear is **eating** his lunch.

envelope

Carly Cat is licking the **envelope**.

eagle

The **eagle** has a sharp beak and sharp claws.

egg

The baby bird comes out of the **egg**.

escalator

Kelly Kangaroo rides down the **escalator**.

earth

The **earth** is round.

elephant

Ellie is an **elephant**.

abcd**ef**ghijklmnopqrstuvwxyz

escaping

The prisoner is **escaping** from jail.

Ff

factory

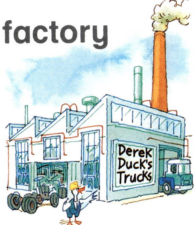

Derek Duck makes trucks in his **factory**.

falling

Sam Squirrel is **falling** off the tree.

family

This is Molly Monkey's **family**.

exercising

Molly is **exercising** on her exercise bike.

fairy

The **fairy** is flying.

farmer

The **farmer** grows corn on his farm.

abcde**f**ghijklmnopqrstuvwxyz

father

Leo Lion is the **father** of the cubs.

field
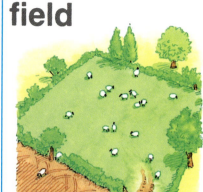
The sheep are grazing in the **field**.

fish

The **fish** is blowing bubbles in his bowl.

feather

Roger Rabbit has a red **feather** in his cap.

filling

Hilda Hippo is **filling** the bath with water.

fishing

Willie Worm is **fishing**.

fence

Sam Squirrel is sitting on the **fence**.

fire engine

The **fire engine** races to the burning fire.

flag

Kelly is waving a **flag**.

abcde**f**ghijklmnopqrstuvwxyz

floating
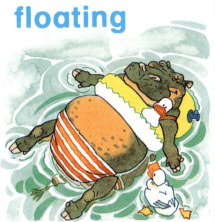
Hilda Hippo is **floating** on top of the water.

fork

Sometimes Boris Bear eats with a **fork**.

fox

The **fox** is stealing some eggs to eat.

flower

A big, pink **flower**.

fountain

Derek Duck is on top of the **fountain**.

frog

Freddie is a fat **frog**.

fly

The **fly** is climbing up the wall.

fruit

A big bowl of **fruit**.

abcdefghijklmnopqrstuvwxyz

Gg

garden

Patsy Pig has a very pretty **garden**.

giant

game

Willie and Millie are playing a **game**.

gate

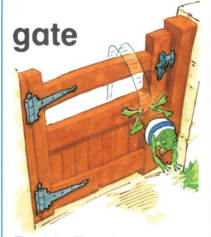

Freddie Frog leaps over the red **gate**.

A jolly **giant**.

garage

Derek Duck drives his car into the **garage**.

ghost

Derek Duck is dressed up as a **ghost**.

giraffe

Gertie is a **giraffe**.

abcdefghijklmnopqrstuvwxyz

girl

Sophie is a **girl**.

glove

Roger Rabbit is wearing a baseball **glove**.

goose

The **goose** is chasing Derek Duck.

glass

A **glass** of lemonade.

goat

The **goat** is chewing Patsy Pig's apron.

gorilla

The **gorilla** beats his chest.

glasses

Willie Worm wears his **glasses** to read.

gold

A chest full of **gold**.

grape
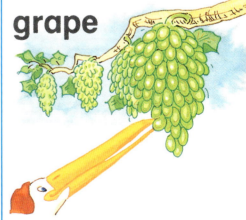
Bill Bird is picking a **grape** to eat.

abcdefghijklmnopqrstuvwxyz

grapefruit

The **grapefruit** is on Boris Bear's plate.

ground
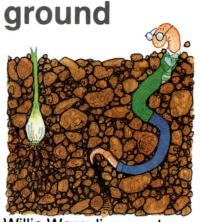
Willie Worm lives under the **ground**.

Hh

grass

Leo Lion is hiding in the tall **grass**.

guitar

Molly sings while she plays her **guitar**.

hamburger

A big, juicy **hamburger**.

grasshopper

The **grasshopper** hops over the grass.

gun

This is Roger Rabbit's toy **gun**.

hammer

The **hammer** knocks the nail into the wood.

26

abcdefg**h**ijklmnopqrstuvwxyz

hamster

The **hamster** is Millie Mouse's friend.

hat

Gertie Giraffe is wearing her best **hat** today.

helmet

Molly Monkey has a **helmet** on her head.

hanging

Molly Monkey is **hanging** by her tail.

hedge
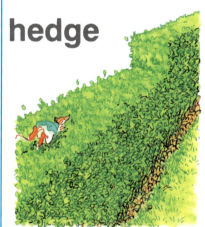
Millie Mouse scampers along the **hedge**.

helping

Millie is **helping** Patsy to hang up the washing.

helicopter

The **helicopter** flies high in the sky.

hiding
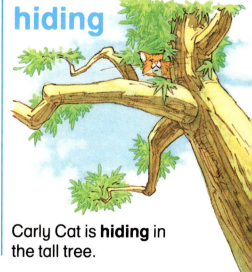
Carly Cat is **hiding** in the tall tree.

27

abcdefg**h**ijklmnopqrstuvwxyz

hill

Dudley Dog is running up the steep **hill**.

holiday
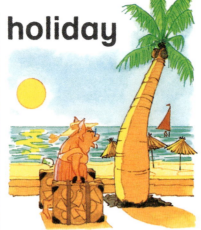
Patsy Pig goes on **holiday** every summer.

horse

The **horse** gallops off with Roger Rabbit.

hippopotamus

Hilda is a happy **hippopotamus**.

honey

A pot of runny **honey**.

hospital
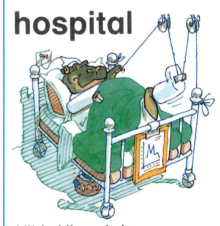
Hilda Hippo is in **hospital**.

hole
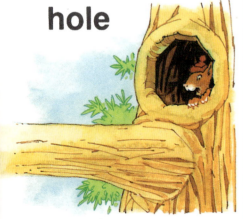
Sam Squirrel peeps out of the **hole**.

hook

The keys are hanging on the **hook**.

house

This is Millie Mouse's little **house**.

abcdefgh**i****j**klmnopqrstuvwxyz

Ii

ice

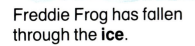

Freddie Frog has fallen through the **ice**.

ice cream

Kelly Kangaroo loves to eat **ice cream**.

insect

A scary **insect** with a big sting.

iron

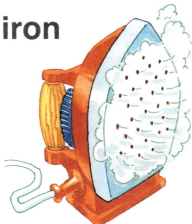

The **iron** is hot.

island

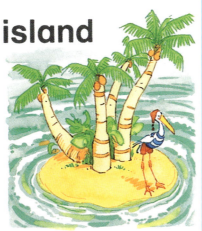

Bill Bird is all alone on the **island**.

Jj

jacket

Boris Bear has a new, striped **jacket**.

jar

There is one sweet left in the **jar**.

29

abcdefghi j k lmnopqrstuvwxyz

jeans

Boris Bear's **jeans** are hanging up to dry.

jug

A **jug** of orange juice.

Kk

jeep

The **jeep** drives over a bumpy road.

jumping

Freddie Frog is **jumping** over the hurdle.

kangaroo

jewels

Patsy Pig wears lots of sparkling **jewels**.

jungle
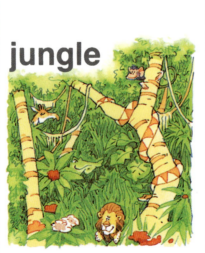
Lots of animals live in the **jungle**.

Kelly is a **kangaroo**.

30

abcdefghij**k**lmnopqrstuvwxyz

kettle

The **kettle** is boiling.

king

The **king** is sitting on his throne.

kite
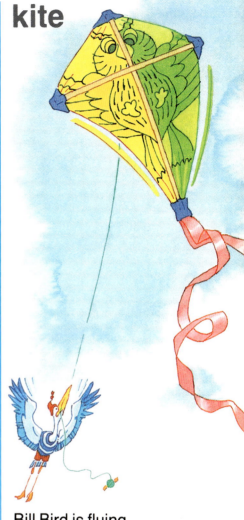
Bill Bird is flying his **kite**.

key

Molly Monkey puts the **key** into the keyhole.

kissing
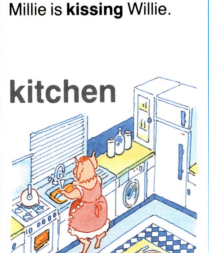
Millie is **kissing** Willie.

kicking

Roger Rabbit is **kicking** the ball.

kitchen
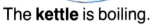
Patsy Pig is working in her **kitchen**.

knife
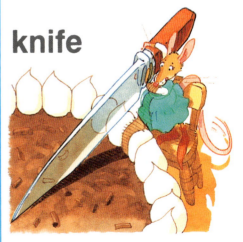
Millie Mouse cuts the cake with a sharp **knife**.

abcdefghijk**l**mnopqrstuvwxyz

Ll

lamb

The **lamb** is chasing a yellow butterfly.

leaf

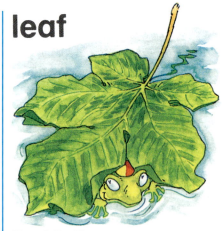

Freddie Frog is hiding under a green **leaf**.

ladder

lamp

Willie Worm has a **lamp** beside his bed.

lemon

The yellow wasp is on the yellow **lemon**.

laughing

letter

Molly Monkey is climbing up the **ladder**.

Roger Rabbit is **laughing** at Derek Duck.

Patsy Pig is writing a **letter** to Boris.

abcdefghijk**lm**nopqrstuvwxyz

lettuce

The caterpillar is nibbling the **lettuce**.

lion

Leo is a handsome **lion**.

Mm

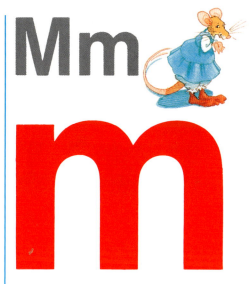

m

lighthouse

Bill Bird is looking out of the **lighthouse**.

lizard

The **lizard** has caught a fly with his tongue.

magician

The **magician** is doing a clever trick.

lollipop

Millie Mouse is licking a red **lollipop**.

man

The **man** is wearing a blue, striped suit.

33

abcdefghijklmnopqrstuvwxyz

map

Derek Duck is looking at a **map**.

matches

Millie is naughty, she is playing with **matches**.

milk

Carly Cat has spilt the **milk** on the floor.

marbles

The glass **marbles** are different colours.

meat

The butcher has all kinds of **meat** in his shop.

mirror

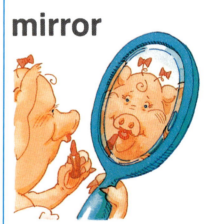

Patsy Pig is looking at herself in the **mirror**.

mask

The **mask** makes Roger look like a monster.

medicine

The baby is going to have her **medicine**.

model

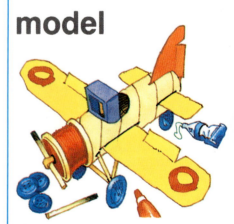

This is Derek Duck's **model** aeroplane.

34

abcdefghijkl**m**nopqrstuvwxyz

money

Boris Bear has lots of **money** in his hand.

mother
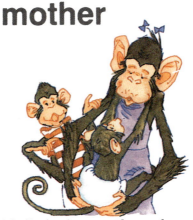
Molly is the **mother** of two little monkeys.

mouse

Millie is a **mouse**.

monkey

Molly is a **monkey**.

mountain

Bill Bird is on top of the high **mountain**.

mug

Boris Bear's **mug** is hanging on the hook.

moon

The **moon** is shining in the dark sky.

mushroom

Freddie Frog is slipping off the **mushroom**.

35

abcdefghijklm**n**opqrstuvwxyz

Nn

needle

Millie Mouse is threading the **needle**.

newspaper

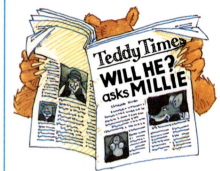

Boris Bear is reading his **newspaper**.

nails

There are lots of **nails** in the box.

nest

The two baby birds are in the **nest**.

nurse

The **nurse** is taking Hilda Hippo's pulse.

necklace

Patsy Pig's **necklace** is around her neck.

net

Willie Worm has caught a fish in his **net**.

nuts

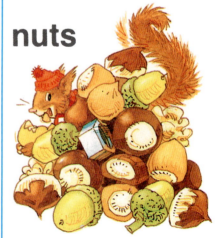

Sam Squirrel has a big pile of **nuts**.

abcdefghijklmn**o**pqrstuvwxyz

Oo

onion

The **onion** is making Millie Mouse cry.

ostrich

octopus

Ollie is an **octopus**.

opening

Patsy Pig is **opening** a can of beans.

The **ostrich** is much bigger than Bill Bird.

office

Willie Worm works hard in his **office**.

orange

Molly Monkey wants to eat the ripe **orange**.

owl

The **owl** is sitting on a branch.

37

abcdefghijklmno**p**qrstuvwxyz

Pp

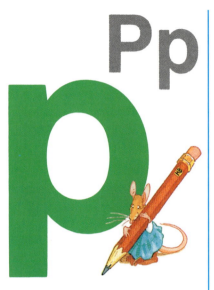

panda

The **panda** is eating a bamboo shoot.

park

Patsy Pig is meeting Boris Bear in the **park**.

painting

Millie is **painting** a picture of Roger.

parachute

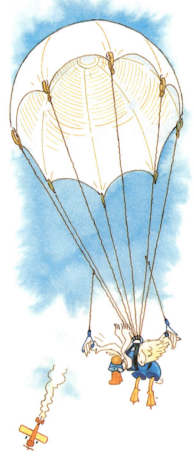

Derek Duck is coming down by **parachute**.

parrot

The **parrot** is swinging on his perch.

pancake

Patsy Pig is tossing a huge **pancake**.

party

The animals are having a wonderful **party**.

abcdefghijklmno**p**qrstuvwxyz

paying

Patsy Pig is **paying** Derek Duck for the food.

peas

Peas in a pod.

photograph

A bad **photograph** of big Boris Bear.

peach

A **peach** on a plate.

pencil

Millie Mouse is drawing with a **pencil**.

piano

Ollie Octopus is good at playing the **piano**.

pears
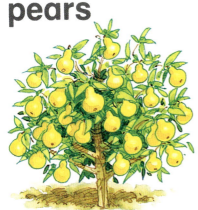
Pears on a pear tree.

penguin

The **penguin** is keeping her chick warm.

picking

Ellie Elephant is **picking** apples off the tree.

abcdefghijklmno p qrstuvwxyz

picnic

Willie and Millie are having a **picnic**.

pigeon
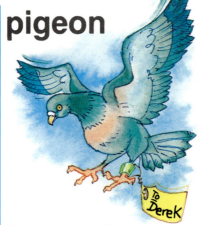
This is Derek Duck's pet **pigeon**.

pins
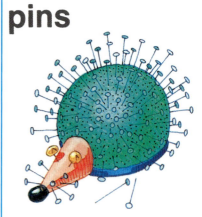
The **pins** are stuck in the pincushion.

pie

A piping hot **pie**.

pillow

Millie Mouse is resting against a soft **pillow**.

pirate

Bill Bird, the **pirate**, is looking for land.

pig

Patsy is a pretty **pig**.

pineapple

Millie Mouse is tasting the **pineapple**.

40

abcdefghijklmno**p**qrstuvwxyz

pizza

A delicious, hot, cheese and tomato **pizza**.

playing

Freddie Frog is **playing** leapfrog with his friend.

postcard

Patsy Pig has sent a **postcard** to Boris Bear.

planting

Patsy Pig is **planting** rows of poppy seeds.

pocket

Millie Mouse is peeping out of the **pocket**.

potatoes

A sack of **potatoes**.

plate

This is Boris Bear's best **plate**.

poppy
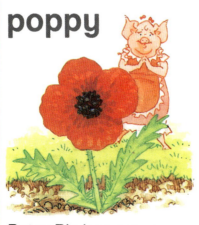
Patsy Pig has grown a beautiful, red **poppy**.

present

Ollie Octopus is opening his **present**.

41

abcdefghijklmno p q rstuvwxyz

princess

The **princess** loves the handsome prince.

puppet

Molly Monkey is playing with her **puppet**.

Qq
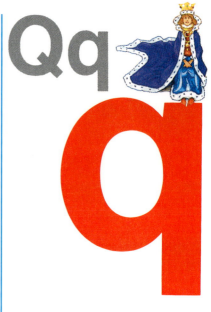

pulling

The cub is **pulling** Leo Lion's tail.

puppy

The **puppy** is chewing Boris Bear's slipper.

quarter

A **quarter** of the pie has been eaten.

pushing

Patsy Pig is **pushing** her piglets in the pram.

queen

The **queen** has a long purple robe.

abcdefghijklmnopqrstuvwxyz

Rr

radiator

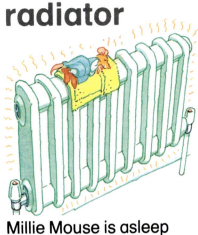

Millie Mouse is asleep on the warm **radiator**.

raining

It is **raining** hard.

rabbit

Roger is a noisy **rabbit**.

radio

Dudley Dog is listening to the **radio**.

racing

Freddie Frog is **racing** against Sam Squirrel.

rainbow

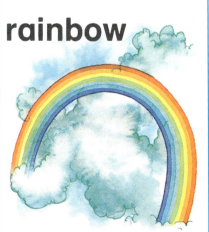

There are seven colours in the **rainbow**.

rat

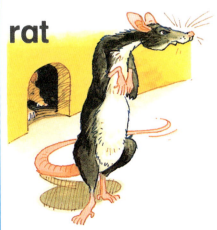

Millie Mouse is hiding from the **rat**.

43

abcdefghijklmnopq**r**stuvwxyz

reading

Willie Worm is **reading** in bed.

ribbons

Gertie Giraffe has lots of **ribbons** in her hair.

river

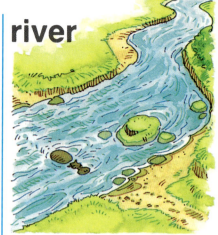

Hilda Hippo is swimming across the **river**.

record

Patsy Pig is playing her favourite **record**.

riding

The cub is **riding** on Leo Lion's back.

road

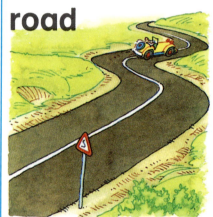

Derek Duck is driving along the winding **road**.

reindeer

Santa's **reindeer** has a red nose.

ring

Patsy Pig is wearing a **ring** on her finger.

robot

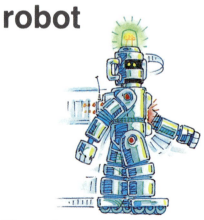

The **robot** can walk and talk.

44

abcdefghijklmnopqrstuvwxyz

rock

Freddie Frog is climbing on to the **rock**.

rocking horse

Millie Mouse is sitting on a **rocking horse**.

rope

Molly Monkey is swinging on a long **rope**.

rocket

The **rocket** blasts off to the moon.

rolling

The snowball is **rolling** away from Dudley Dog.

roof

Sam Squirrel is running up the steep **roof**.

rose

Patsy Pig is smelling the red **rose**.

45

abcdefghijkl mnopq**r****s**tuvwxyz

rowing

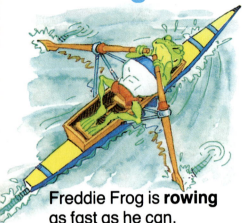

Freddie Frog is **rowing** as fast as he can.

Ss

sandals

A pair of red **sandals**.

ruler

Molly is measuring her tail with a **ruler**.

sailor

Ollie Octopus is a **sailor**.

sandwich

A tomato, ham and lettuce **sandwich** for Boris.

running

Roger Rabbit is **running** as fast as he can.

sand

Hilda Hippo is buried in the **sand**.

sausages

Dudley Dog has stolen the **sausages**.

46

abcdefghijklmnopqr**s**tuvwxyz

saw

A sharp, shiny **saw**.

school

Willie Worm goes to **school** to learn.

seal

The **seal** is sunbathing on a rock.

scarecrow

The **scarecrow** doesn't scare Bill Bird.

scissors

Molly Monkey cuts the paper with **scissors**.

sea
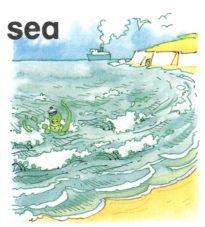
Ollie Octopus is swimming in the blue **sea**.

sewing

Patsy Pig is **sewing** on a button for Boris.

shadow

Gertie Giraffe looks at her **shadow**.

abcdefghijkr**s**tuvwxyz

sheep

The **sheep** has two lambs.

shirt

Boris Bear's striped **shirt** is on a hanger.

shorts

Roger Rabbit is wearing his red **shorts**.

shell

Willie Worm has found a **shell** on the beach.

shoe

Millie Mouse is asleep in Boris Bear's **shoe**.

shouting

Molly Monkey is **shouting** at Derek Duck.

ship

The **ship** is sailing across the blue sea.

shopping

Kelly Kangaroo has been **shopping** today.

shower

Hilda Hippo is having a nice hot **shower**.

48

abcdefghijklmnopqr**s**tuvwxyz

signpost

The **signpost** shows Millie the way to go home.

skeleton
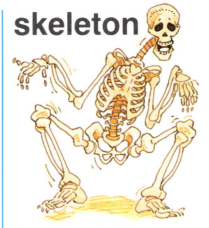
A smiling **skeleton**.

slide
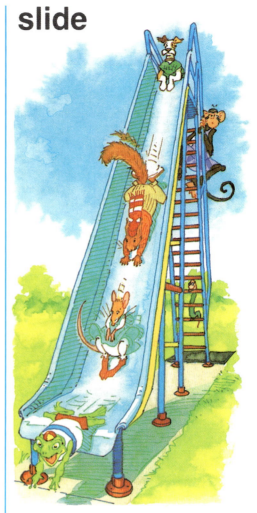
The animals are sliding down the **slide**.

sink

Freddie Frog is swimming in the **sink**.

skiing

Derek Duck is **skiing**.

skates

These are Molly Monkey's new roller **skates**.

sleeping

Boris Bear is **sleeping** very soundly.

slippers

Freddie Frog jumps into Boris Bear's **slippers**.

abcdefghijklmnopqr**s**tuvwxyz

smelling

Boris Bear is **smelling** the apple pie.

snow

Sam Squirrel is covered with **snow**.

soap

The pink **soap** is in the soap dish.

snail

The **snail** is making a slippery trail.

snowman
Millie Mouse is looking up at the **snowman**.

socks
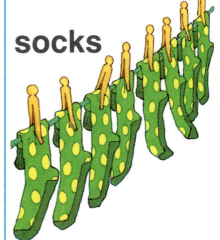
Ollie Octopus's **socks** are hanging up to dry.

snake
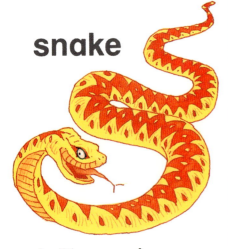
A slithery **snake**.

soldier

Roger Rabbit is dressed up as a **soldier**.

50

abcdefghijkqr**s**tuvwxyz

spade

Willie Worm is sleeping beside the **spade**.

splashing

Freddie Frog is **splashing** Derek Duck.

stairs
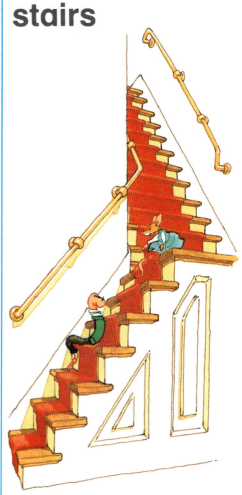
Willie and Millie are climbing up the **stairs**.

spider

A scary, hairy **spider**.

spoon

Molly Monkey is feeding her baby with a **spoon**.

squirrel
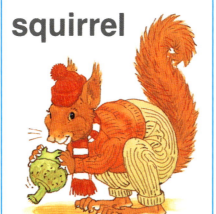
Sam is a hungry **squirrel**.

stamp

There is a picture of Leo Lion on the **stamp**.

abcdefghijklmnopqr**s**tuvwxyz

star

The **star** shines brightly in the sky at night.

stool

Millie Mouse is sitting on a green **stool**.

string

Carly Cat is unwinding the ball of **string**.

station

Patsy Pig is waiting at the **station** for a train.

straw

Molly Monkey drinks through a striped **straw**.

submarine

The **submarine** is deep under the sea.

stealing

The thief is **stealing** some jewels.

strawberries

A plate of delicious, red **strawberries**.

sun

The hot **sun** shines down on the yellow sand.

abcdefghijklmnopqr**s**tuvwxyz

sunglasses

Patsy wears **sunglasses** in the hot sunshine.

swan

The **swan** carries her baby on her back.

swimming

Freddie is **swimming** as fast as he can.

swing

Molly Monkey is swinging on the **swing**.

sword

Roger Rabbit is playing with his toy **sword**.

Tt

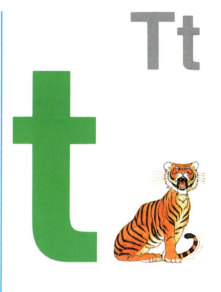

table

Dudley Dog is lying under the **table**.

tadpoles

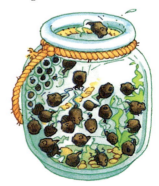

The jar is full of tiny **tadpoles**.

53

abcdefghijklmnopqrs**t**uvwxyz

tail

Sam Squirrel has a long, bushy **tail**.

teddy bear

The **teddy bear** is blue and white.

television

Carly Cat is watching **television**.

taxi

Gertie Giraffe is riding in the **taxi**.

teeth
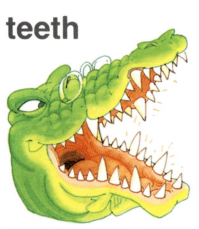
Old Croc has lots of sharp **teeth**.

tent

Dudley Dog is fast asleep in his green **tent**.

teacher

The **teacher** is writing on the board.

telephone

Patsy Pig is talking on the **telephone**.

thief

The **thief** is climbing out of the window.

abcdefghijklmnopqrs**t**uvwxyz

thimble

Patsy Pig has a **thimble** on her finger.

tie

Willie Worm is wearing a green and white **tie**.

toothbrush

Old Croc's **toothbrush** has lots of bristles.

throwing

tiger

The **tiger** is roaring.

toothpaste

Millie Mouse squeezes the tube of **toothpaste**.

Roger Rabbit is **throwing** the ball into the air.

tomato

A juicy, red **tomato**.

towel

Hilda Hippo dries herself with a huge **towel**.

55

abcdefghijklmnopqrs**t**uvwxyz

toys

There are lots of **toys** on the floor.

train

The **train** speeds down the railway track.

tricycle
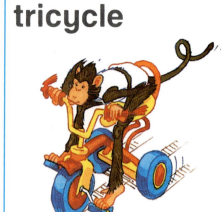
The baby monkey is riding a **tricycle**.

tractor

Derek Duck is driving a **tractor**.

tree

trousers

Boris Bear has a patch on his **trousers**.

traffic lights

The **traffic lights** have changed to green.

Bill Bird is hiding behind the fir **tree**.

truck

The **truck** is dumping the dirt.

abcdefghijklmnopqrs**t**uvwxyz

trumpet

Ollie Octopus is blowing his **trumpet**.

T-shirt

Kelly Kangaroo is wearing a big **T-shirt**.

turkey

A gobbling **turkey**.

trunk

Millie Mouse sits on Ellie Elephant's **trunk**.

tulips

Two **tulips** in a vase.

tunnel
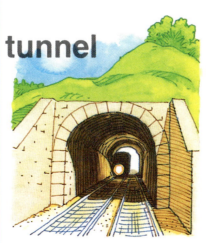
The train is going through a dark **tunnel**.

twins

These girls are **twins**.

typewriter

Willie Worm is typing on his **typewriter**.

abcdefghijklmnopqrst u v wxyz

Uu

Vv

violin

Molly Monkey is playing the **violin** softly.

u

V

umbrella

The big **umbrella** keeps Derek Duck dry.

vacuum cleaner

Patsy cleans the carpet with a **vacuum cleaner**.

volcano

undressing

Molly Monkey is **undressing**.

vegetables

Willie Worm is hiding in a pile of **vegetables**.

Hot rocks and lava burst out of the **volcano**.

abcdefghijklmnopqrstuv**w**xyz

Ww

washing

Molly Monkey is **washing** her baby.

watch

Boris Bear is wearing a **watch** on his wrist.

walking

Leo Lion is out **walking** with his cubs.

washing machine

Willie Worm's tie is in the **washing machine**.

whale

wall

Sam Squirrel is running along the brick **wall**.

wasp

The **wasp** has stung Roger Rabbit.

The **whale** gives Ollie Octopus a ride on his back.

59

abcdefghijklmnopqrstuv**w**xyz

wheel

Derek Duck has taken the **wheel** off his car.

whiskers

Leo Lion has beautiful, long **whiskers**.

whistle

Roger Rabbit is blowing his **whistle** loudly.

windmill

Bill Bird lands on top of the **windmill**.

window

Carly Cat looks out of the **window**.

witch

The **witch** flies around on her broomstick.

wood
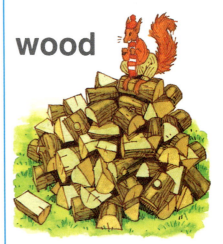
Sam Squirrel sits on the pile of **wood**.

writing
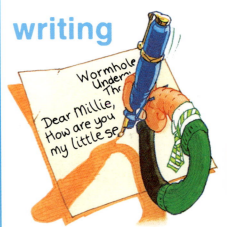
Willie Worm is **writing** a letter to Millie Mouse.

abcdefghijklmnopqrstuvw**xyz**

Xx Yy Zz

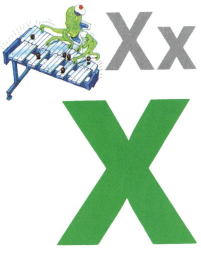

x y z

x-ray
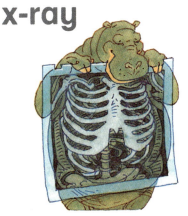
Hilda Hippo holds up an **x-ray** of herself.

yacht
Derek Duck is sailing his **yacht**.

zebra
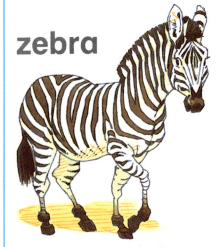
The **zebra** has black and white stripes.

xylophone

Ollie Octopus is playing the **xylophone**.

yawning

Leo Lion is **yawning**.

zoo

The Word Gang are at the **zoo**.

61

Extra Words

Parts of the body

Colours

Numbers

1 one
2 two
3 three
4 four
5 five
6 six
7 seven
8 eight
9 nine
10 ten

Shapes

square, circle, oval, triangle, rectangle, star

Designer: Edward Kinsey

First published in Great Britain in 1988 by
Conran Octopus

This edition published in 2008 by Bounty Books,
a division of Octopus Publishing Group Ltd
2 - 4 Heron Quays, London E14 4JP
www.octopusbooks.co.uk

An Hachette Livre UK Company
www.hachettelivre.co.uk

Copyright © Octopus Publishing Group Ltd 2008

All rights reserved. No part of this work may be reproduced or utilized in
any form or by any means, electronic or mechanical, including photocopying,
recording or by any information storage and retrieval system, without the
prior written permission of the publisher

ISBN: 978-0-75371-816-2

A CIP catalogue record for this book is available from the British Library

Printed and bound in China